GENES
"M" IS FOR "

Primo Scagnetti

HELLO
CARLO
PRESS

twitter.com/primoscagnetti
@PrimoScagnetti

GENESIS:
"M" IS FOR "MAMA"

INTRODUCTION

Genesis released fifteen studio albums
between 1969 and 1997. They did this with
three lead singers (the last one for just one
album). Their first singer left in 1975, and
the drummer they hired in August of 1970
took over singing while retaining sole
drumming duties (in the studio), thus
becoming the second lead singer. He sang
lead on their next eight albums, the last one
being released in 1991. The two remaining
guys found a new guy to sing, and they
released a final gasp of an album in 1997.

They got back together with their second
singer for a tour in 2007, and once again in
2022 for what appears to be a final farewell
tour.

This project simply pairs the alphabet with
26 corresponding songs from the second part
of the Phil Collins era (the five studio albums
released between 1980-1991). Their
penultimate album *INVISIBLE TOUCH* and
its accompanying tour were worldwide
successes, and the title track would prove to
be their only No. 1 single in the United
States. They were able to release one more

album with Collins in 1991, entitled *WE CAN'T DANCE.*

DUKE
MAR 1980

ABACAB
SEP 1981

GENESIS
OCT 1983

INVISIBLE TOUCH
JUN 1986

WE CAN'T DANCE
NOV 1991

Enjoy...

- P.S., March 2023

Aa

is for
"**A**BACAB"

FROM THE STUDIO ALBUM:

ABACAB
(1981)

Bb

is for
"BEHIND
THE LINES"

FROM THE STUDIO ALBUM:

DUKE
(1980)

NOTE:
Collins would do his own cover version of
"Behind the Lines" for his 1981 debut solo
album, *FACE VALUE.*

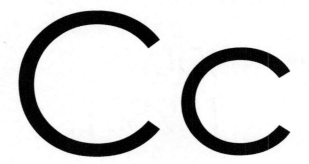

is for

"I

CAN'T

DANCE"

WE CAN'T DANCE (1991)

Dd

is for
"**D**OMINO"

FROM THE STUDIO ALBUM:

INVISIBLE TOUCH (1986)

NOTE:
"DOMINO" is divided into two parts, "IN
THE GLOW OF THE NIGHT" and "THE
LAST DOMINO".

Ee

is for

"DUK**E**'S
END"

FROM THE STUDIO ALBUM:

DUKE
(1980)

Ff

is for
"**F**ADING
LIGHTS"

FROM THE STUDIO ALBUM:

WE CAN'T DANCE (1991)

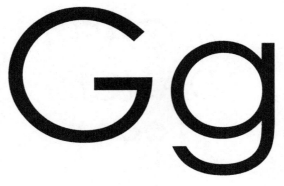

is for

"IT'S
GONNA
GET BETTER"

FROM THE STUDIO ALBUM:

GENESIS
(1983)

is for
"**H**OME
BY THE SEA"

FROM THE STUDIO ALBUM:

GENESIS
(1983)

Ii

is for
"**I**NVISIBLE
TOUCH"

FROM THE STUDIO ALBUM:

INVISIBLE TOUCH (1986)

Jj

is for

"JUST A JOB
TO DO"

FROM THE STUDIO ALBUM:

GENESIS
(1983)

Kk

is for
"**K**EEP
IT
DAR**K**"

FROM THE STUDIO ALBUM:

ABACAB
(1981)

Ll

is for
"LAND
OF CONFUSION"

FROM THE STUDIO ALBUM:

INVISIBLE TOUCH (1986)

Mm

is for
"**MAMA**"

FROM THE STUDIO ALBUM:

GENESIS
(1983)

Nn

is for
"NO SON
OF MINE"

FROM THE STUDIO ALBUM:

WE CAN'T DANCE (1991)

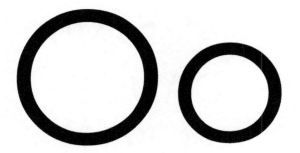

is for

"M A N

ON

THE CORNER"

FROM THE STUDIO ALBUM:

ABACAB
(1981)

Pp

is for
"PLEASE
DON'T ASK"

FROM THE STUDIO ALBUM:

DUKE
(1980)

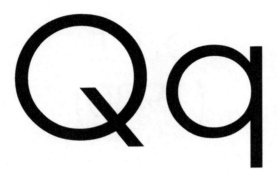

is for

*"...**q**uestions..."*

FROM THE SONG:
"IN TOO DEEP"

FROM THE STUDIO ALBUM:

INVISIBLE TOUCH (1986)

NOTE:

Famously featured in the 2000 film *AMERICAN PSYCHO,* the character of Patrick Bateman delivers a monologue about the 1980's discography of Genesis. He holds up a CD of Collins' 1985 solo album *NO JACKET REQUIRED* as he discusses Genesis, giving special praise to the song "IN TOO DEEP" and what it means to him. "Sussudio" features in the following scene as he entertains his "guests". Bret Easton Ellis, the author of the novel *AMERICAN PSCYHO,* devotes a whole chapter to Genesis (as he does with Whitney Houston and Huey Lewis and The News). However, the chapter about Genesis contains several factual errors about the band, which is kind of amusing.

Rr

is for

"ANOTHER
RECORD"

FROM THE STUDIO ALBUM:

ABACAB
(1981)

Ss

is for
"SILVER
RAINBOW"

FROM THE STUDIO ALBUM:

GENESIS
(1983)

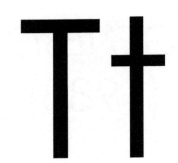

is for
"TONIGHT,
TONIGHT,
TONIGHT"

FROM THE STUDIO ALBUM:

INVISIBLE
TOUCH
(1986)

Uu

is for
"D**U**CHESS"

FROM THE STUDIO ALBUM:

DUKE
(1980)

is for

"GUIDE

VOCAL"

FROM THE STUDIO ALBUM:

DUKE
(1980)

is for
"**W**HO
DUNNIT**?**"

FROM THE STUDIO ALBUM:

ABACAB
(1981)

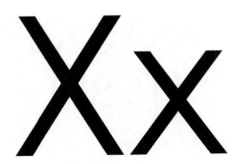

is for

"...e**X**tinct..."

FROM THE SONG:
"CUL-DE-SAC"

FROM THE STUDIO ALBUM:

DUKE
(1980)

Yy

is for

"DREAMING WHILE

YOU SLEEP"

WE CAN'T DANCE (1991)

Zz

is for

"THE

BRAZILIAN"

FROM THE STUDIO ALBUM:

INVISIBLE TOUCH (1986)

STUDIO ALBUM
<u>DISCOGRAPHY</u>
(1969 - 1997)

FROM GENESIS
TO REVELATION
1969

TRESPASS
1970

NURSERY CRYME
1971

FOXTROT
1972

SELLING ENGLAND
BY THE POUND
1973

THE LAMB LIES
DOWN ON BROADWAY
1974

A TRICK OF THE TAIL
1976

WIND & WUTHERING
1976

AND THEN THERE WERE THREE
1978

DUKE
1980

ABACAB
1981

GENESIS
1983

INVISIBLE TOUCH
1986

WE CAN'T DANCE
1991

CALLING ALL STATIONS
1997

PLAYLIST

"ABACAB"

"BEHIND THE LINES"

"I CAN'T DANCE"

"DOMINO"

"DUKE'S END"

"FADING LIGHTS"

"IT'S GONNA
GET BETTER"

"HOME BY THE SEA"

"INVISIBLE TOUCH"

"JUST A JOB TO DO"

"KEEP IT DARK"

"LAND OF CONFUSION"

"MAMA"

"NO SON OF MINE"

"MAN ON THE CORNER"

"PLEASE DON'T ASK"

"IN TOO DEEP"

"ANOTHER RECORD"

"SILVER RAINBOW"

"TONIGHT,
TONIGHT, TONIGHT"

"DUCHESS"

"GUIDE VOCAL"

"WHO DUNNIT?"

"CUL-DE-SAC"

"DREAMING
WHILE YOU SLEEP"

"THE BRAZILIAN"

Printed in Great Britain
by Amazon

27270810R00036